LIGHTNING BOLT BOOKS™

How Submarines Work

Walt Brody

Lerner Publications • Minneapolis

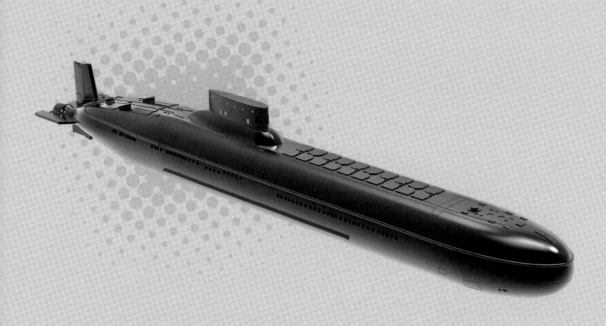

Lerner Publications Company
A division of Lerner Publishing Group, Inc.
241 First Avenue North
Minneapolis, MN 55401 USA

For reading levels and more information, look up this title at www.lernerbooks.com.

Library of Congress Cataloging-in-Publication Data

Names: Brody, Walt, 1978- author.
Title: How submarines work / Walt Brody.
Description: Minneapolis : Lerner Publications, [2019] | Series: Lightning bolt books: military machines | Includes index. | Audience: Grades K-3. | Audience: Ages 6-9.
Identifiers: LCCN 2018040878 (print) | LCCN 2018041149 (ebook) | ISBN 9781541556584 (eb pdf) | ISBN 9781541555686 (lb : alk. paper)
Subjects: LCSH: Submarines (Ships)—Juvenile literature.
Classification: LCC VM365 (ebook) | LCC VM365 .B86 2019 (print) | DDC 623.825/7—dc23

LC record available at https://lccn.loc.gov/2018040878

Manufactured in the United States of America
1-46023-43346-12/18/2018

Table of Contents

The Diving Submarine

Many ships move on the surface of the ocean. But submarines can move deep under the water's surface.

Submarines are long and narrow watercraft. The front is round to help it move underwater. The hull is the outside of the submarine.

USS *Ohio* class submarines are 515 feet (157 m) long.

The captain is in charge of a submarine and its officers. Officers are in charge of different parts of the ship. The officers give the crew orders.

The captain shows respect to his crew by saluting.

Crew members make sure the submarine is ready to dive.

It takes many crew members to run a military submarine. Each crew member has a job. Some work with sonar or weapons. Other crew members may cook.

A History of Submarines

Cornelis Drebbel built submarines in 1620. The largest one held a crew of sixteen. The crew rowed oars to move the submarine.

These submarines from the United States fought during World War I.

Submarines were a major part of World War I (1914-1918). They attacked enemy ships and laid mines in the water.

The first nuclear submarine was the USS *Nautilus*.

Nuclear submarines were first built in the 1950s.

These submarines use nuclear energy for power. The energy helps them stay underwater longer than other submarines.

Parts of a Submarine

The back of a submarine has a propeller. The propeller spins to move the submarine. Rudders turn the watercraft.

Modern submarines may stay underwater for ninety days at a time.

Large ballast tanks fill with water to make the submarine heavier. This causes it to sink below the surface of the sea.

Torpedoes are the main weapons of a military submarine. A torpedo is an underwater missile. Submarines can fire torpedoes at targets that are far away.

Torpedoes can destroy submarines and ships on the surface.

Military submarines do not have windows. They use sonar to form a picture of the ocean around them. They can also listen to sounds made by other ships in the water.

A sailor checks a submarine's sonar.

A periscope can turn in all directions.

Crew members use a periscope to look above the surface of the water. The periscope lets the crew see ships on the surface.

Submarines in Action

The US Navy uses submarines because they can hide easily underwater. A hidden submarine can make a sneak attack. Submarines can hide almost anywhere in the ocean.

Sailors tie the USS *Indiana* to a dock.

There are about 540 military submarines worldwide. The United States has sixty-six active submarines. **That's more submarines than any other country has.**

Submarines do other things too. When military submarines finish doing their jobs, they sometimes become museums for people to tour.

The USS *Bowfin* fought in World War II (1939–1945), and now it is a museum you can visit.

Scientists think that future submarines could travel more than 230 miles (370 km) per hour!

In the future, submarines might be able to go faster than ever. Scientists are planning a submarine that makes a bubble of air around itself. It will use this bubble to go superfast.

Submarine Diagram

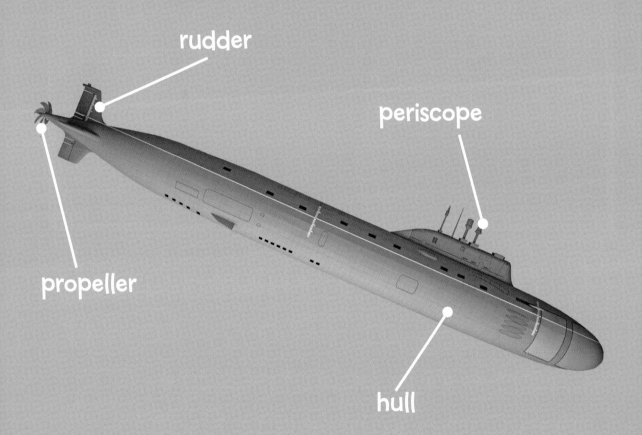

rudder

periscope

propeller

hull

Submarine Facts

- Some military submarines carry nuclear missiles. The submarines fire the missiles into the air. These missiles can travel thousands of miles to their target.

- In 1776, David Bushnell made a submarine out of wood. He named it the *Turtle*. It held only one person.

- Military submarines are big. They need a lot of crew members. USS *Ohio* class submarines have 144 crew members and fifteen officers.

Glossary

ballast tank: a tank that fills with water allowing a submarine to dive

crew: a group of people that runs a submarine

mine: a bomb placed underground or in the water

nuclear energy: energy created by splitting an atom

officer: a crew member who is in charge of other crew members

periscope: a tube with mirrors used to see above the surface of the water

rudder: a flat piece of metal used to steer a submarine

sonar: a system that uses sound to find objects underwater

Further Reading

Allen, Kenny. *Submarines*. New York: Gareth Stevens, 2013.

Boothroyd, Jennifer. *Inside the US Navy*. Minneapolis: Lerner Publications, 2018.

Kidzsearch: Navy Facts for Kids
https://wiki.kidzsearch.com/wiki/Navy

Mattern, Joanne. *How Things Work: Submarines*. New York: Children's Press, 2016.

Science for Kids: Submarine Facts
http://www.scienceforkidsclub.com/submarines.html

Science Kids: Submarine Facts for Kids
http://www.sciencekids.co.nz/sciencefacts/vehicles/submarines.html

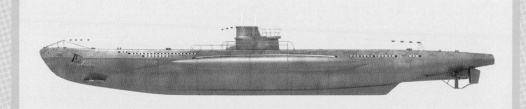

Index

Photo Acknowledgments

Image credits: rimira/Shutterstock.com, p. 2; Stocktrek Images/Getty Images, p. 4; US Navy, p. 5; Amanda R. Gray/US Navy, p. 6; Darryl Wood/US Navy, p. 7; Regional Archive-Alkmaar, p. 8; Naval History and Heritage Command, pp. 9, 10; UMB-O/Shutterstock.com, p. 11; General Dynamics Electric Boat/US Navy, p. 12; Alexander Gamble/US Navy, p. 13; MARTIN BUREAU/AFP/Getty Images, p. 14; Daniel Hinton/US Navy, p. 15; James Kimber/US Navy, p. 16; Sonja Wickard/US Navy, p. 17; Ritu Manoj Jethani/Shutterstock.com, p. 18; irisphoto1/Shutterstock.com, p. 19; kai celvin/Shutterstock.com, p. 20; Nerthuz/Getty Images, p. 23.

Cover Image: Chris Oxley/US Navy.

Main body text set in Billy Infant regular 28/36. Typeface provided by SparkType.